WASHINGTON

in words and pictures

BY DENNIS B. FRADIN

ILLUSTRATIONS BY RICHARD WAHL

MAPS BY LEN W. MEENTS

Consultant
Eugene Friese, Director
Learning Resources
Highline Public Schools

 CHILDRENS PRESS, CHICAGO

Dedication: For my aunt, Esther Greenberg

Olympic National Park

Library of Congress Cataloging in Publication Data

Fradin, Dennis B
  Washington in words and pictures.

  Includes indexes.
  SUMMARY: Presents a brief history and description
of the Evergreen State.
  1. Washington (State) — Juvenile literature.
[1. Washington (State)]   I. Wahl, Richard,
1939- II. Meents, Len W.   III. Title.
F891.3.F72   979.7   80-14745
ISBN 0-516-03947-4

  3 4 5 6 7 8 9 10 11 12 R 87 86 85 84 83 82

Picture Acknowledgments:
DEPARTMENT OF INTERIOR: NATIONAL PARK SERVICE—Cover, 33,
M. Woodbridge Williams, 2, 19 (right); W.S. Keller, 32, 43 (right)
NATIONAL PARK SERVICE: PACIFIC NORTHWEST REGION—4 (right
and below), 12 (above), 21, 23, 24 (right and left), 28, 34, 35 (left), 38, 40,
41, 43 (left)
WIDE WORLD PHOTOS—20
NATIONAL PARK SERVICE: FORT VANCOUVER NATIONAL HISTORIC
SITE—12 (right-top and bottom), 35 (above)
STATE OF WASHINGTON: DEPARTMENT OF NATURAL
RESOURCES—17, 22
BOEING COMPANY—19 (left)
TILLICUM TOURS SERVICE—42
SEATTLE CHAMBER OF COMMERCE—25
SPOKANE CHAMBER OF COMMERCE—29, 39
STATE OF WASHINGTON: DEPARTMENT OF FISHERIES—30, 31
COVER—Mount Rainier from White Pass

Washington

The state of Washington (WAW • shing • ton) was named after the first president of the United States, George Washington. Washington is in the northwest. It is on the coast of the Pacific (pah • SIH • fick) Ocean.

Salmon are caught in the state's waters. Wood and wood products come from Washington forests. Ships and airplanes are built here. Wheat and many other crops are grown in Washington. This state has all these things and much more.

Do you know which state grows the most apples? Do you know where the biggest concrete dam in the United States is? Do you know where the most aluminum is made? As you will learn, the answer to these questions is Washington—the Evergreen State.

Millions of years ago, dinosaurs ruled the land. Their bones have been found in Washington. They lived and died long before there were people in Washington.

For millions of years the land was changing. Volcanoes spat fire high into the air. The earth shook as mountains were pushed from the ground. From time to time, oceans covered the land.

Right: Hoh Glacier
Below: Nisqually Glacier terminus

About a million years ago the weather turned colder. The Ice Age began. Mountains of ice, called *glaciers* (GLAY • sherz), covered the land.

The glaciers left some gifts for Washington. Glaciers ground up rocks into good soil and spread that soil over the land. Glaciers also carved big holes in the ground. Those holes later filled with water and became lakes. The Ice Age ended. But not all the glaciers melted. There is still much glacial ice in the mountains of Washington.

The first people came to Washington at least 10,000 years ago. The early people made stone tools and weapons. They hunted deer and caught fish. They made paintings in caves and cliffs.

These early people were probably related to the Indians who came later.

Many tribes of Indians lived in Washington. These Indians are often thought of as belonging to two groups. The "Canoe" Indians lived in the western half of Washington. They made canoes that were sometimes 60 feet long. They fished for salmon. They lived in wooden houses. They carved wooden masks. Some of the "Canoe" tribes were the Chinook (shin • NOOK), Nooksack, and Nisqually (niss • KWALL • ee).

The Indians in the eastern half of Washington are often called the "Horse" Indians. They hunted deer on horseback. The "Horse" Indians lived in *tepees*—tents made out of animal skins. The tepees were carried on horseback as the Indians moved from place to place. The Spokane (spoh • CAN), Nez Percé (NEZ PURS), Okanogan (oh • KAHN • uh • gan), and Yakima (YOCK • ih • ma) were some of the "Horse" Indian tribes.

The first explorers in Washington worked for the king of Spain. In 1592 Juan de Fuca (WAWN dih FOO • kah) may have sailed up the coast of Washington. Spain ruled in California, south of Washington. Other Spanish explorers came from California. In 1774 Juan Perez (WAWN pair • EZ) sailed along the Washington coast. He saw a snow-capped peak. Later it was named Mount Olympus (oh • LIM • pus). In 1775 two Spanish explorers were the first known to walk on Washington soil. One was named Bruno Heceta (HECK • e • tah). The other had a long name, Juan Francisco de la Bodega y Quadra (WAWN fran • SISS • koh thee lah boh • DAY • gah ee KWAD • drah). They landed near Point Grenville in two boats. They claimed the land for the king of Spain.

These early explorers were not interested in settling this land. They were looking for gold. They were also looking for a water route across America.

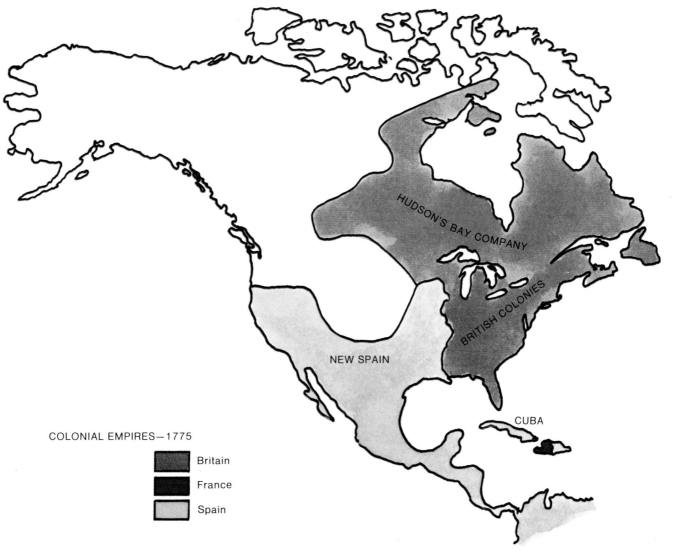

COLONIAL EMPIRES—1775

Britain

France

Spain

The English were also looking for a water route across America. They wanted gold, too.

In 1778 the English explorer James Cook came. He made maps of the Washington coast. A few years later the English explorer George Vancouver (van • KOO • ver) also explored the Washington coast.

Meanwhile, a new country had been formed—the United States of America. Americans came to Washington. In 1792 Robert Gray reached the Columbia River and claimed Washington for the United States. In 1805 the Americans Meriwether Lewis and William Clark explored Washington. They met with friendly Nez Percé Indians. They canoed down the Columbia River and learned about the land.

The Spanish did not find gold in Washington. And they did not find a water route across America. So they lost interest in Washington. But the Americans and the English stayed. They had found a treasure in Washington: animal furs. Countless beavers lived in the rivers and streams. Sea otters lived along the Pacific Ocean. The fur of one sea otter could be sold for as much as two thousand dollars. Money could be made from furs.

English and American men traded with the Indians for furs. In 1810 the English built a fur-trading post near where Spokane stands today. It was called Spokane House. In 1811 the American fur trader John Jacob Astor built Fort Okanogan. This became the first American settlement in Washington.

In 1818 England and the United States agreed that *both* countries could trade in the Oregon (OR • ih • gon) Country. The Oregon Country included Washington.

Above: John McLoughlin
Top right: Reconstruction of bastion and stockade
of Fort Vancouver
Bottom right: Artist's drawing of Fort Vancouver
as it may have looked about 1845

For the English, Dr. John McLoughlin (mick • LOFF •
lin) built Fort Vancouver in 1825. It was on the north
bank of the Columbia River. This fort grew into
Washington's first town—Vancouver. John McLoughlin
ruled like a king over traders and Indians in the
Columbia Valley. He had long white hair and was a very
tall man. The Indians called him the "White-Headed Eagle."

During the 1840s, many Americans went West.
Families went in covered wagons over the Oregon Trail.
A man named George W. Bush traveled with some

OREGON TRAIL—mid 1800s

friends on the Oregon Trail. Bush helped many poor
families by giving them food. They reached what is now
the state of Oregon. George W. Bush was turned away.
He was black. Black people were not permitted to settle
there. The people remembered how George Bush had
helped them. They left Oregon and went farther north to
Washington. They founded Tumwater—the first town in
Washington founded by Americans.

More and more American settlers came to
Washington. They didn't want to share the land with
England any longer. In 1846, by a treaty, Washington
became part of the United States. It wasn't a state yet.
At first it was part of the Oregon Territory. In 1853,
Washington became a separate territory.

With his wife, an American named Dr. Marcus Whitman founded a mission near Walla Walla. At the mission Indians were taught about farming and the Christian religion. The Whitmans also worked to bring new settlers into Washington.

The Indians grew angry at these settlers, including the Whitmans. Settlers were taking over their lands. Indians also were dying of diseases that settlers had brought. In November of 1847 angry Indians killed the Whitmans and a number of others at the mission.

Isaac I. Stevens was the first governor of the Washington Territory. He made treaties with some Indians. Indians were forced to give up their lands.

The "Canoe" Indians gave up their lands more willingly. But the "Horse" Indians in the east were ready to fight. In May of 1855 Governor Stevens called a meeting at Walla Walla. Over 6000 angry "Horse" Indians gathered. "Kill the white men!" said some Indians. Chief Lawyer of the Nez Percé kept the Indians from killing Governor Stevens. Chief Lawyer talked the other Indians into signing the treaty.

The signing of a paper couldn't stop the Indians from fighting. They fought the settlers between 1855 and 1858. The Indian leader was Kamiakin (kah • me • AH • kin), chief of the Yakima. The Indians attacked settlers. They won battles in the Simcoe Valley. They beat U.S. soldiers near Rosalia (roh • ZAL • ee • yah).

This was a bad time in Washington history. Settlers feared Indian arrows, day and night. Indians—such as Chief Quiemuth (KWEE • mith)—were murdered by the settlers. Finally, the Indian Wars ended when 700 soldiers overcame the Indians near Four Lakes. The horses of the Indians were shot so that they could no longer fight on horseback. The Indians had to go live on reservations.

With the Indian Wars ended, more people came to Washington. Many came to farm. Wheat became a big crop. Farmers also raised cattle and sheep.

Loggers also came to Washington. They cut down pine trees. They chopped down Douglas firs. Few people worried about all the tree-cutting. There were many forests in Washington. It seemed that there would always be enough trees.

Above: Sheep grazing
Top left: Wheat field
Bottom left: Sawmill

By 1883 the railroad had crossed Washington, linking it with the eastern United States. More families came. Between the years 1880 and 1890 the population of Washington grew from about 75,000 to about 337,000. Washington had enough people to become a state.

Washington became the 42nd state on November 11, 1889. The capital was made at Olympia (oh • LIM • pyah). Washington became known as the *Evergreen State* because of its forests of fir trees.

Between 1890 and 1900 thousands of Washington farmers caught "apple fever." The good rich soil and weather of Washington were perfect for growing apples. Besides apples, farmers began to grow peaches, pears, and other fruit. And wheat was still a big crop.

By the 1900s, Washington became a big farming, fishing, and timber state. Manufacturing—making things—became important. Seattle and Tacoma (tah • COH • mah) became shipbuilding cities. During World War I (1914-1918), the shipyards of Washington built boats for the United States Navy.

In 1916, William Boeing (BOH • ing) began building airplanes in Seattle. The Boeing Company grew into one of the main airplane builders in the United States. During World War II (1939-1945), hundreds of airplanes were built in Washington.

Above: Logs in lake formed by waters held back
by Grand Coulee Dam
Left: Aircraft assembly line

Eastern Washington did not have enough rain for
crops. Then Grand Coulee (KOO • lee) Dam was
completed in 1942. This dam holds water from the
Columbia River. Thanks to the Grand Coulee Dam, land
that was almost like a desert now has many farms.
Bringing water to places where it is needed is called
irrigation (ear • ih • GAY • shun). In the 1950s and 1960s,
other dams were built on the Columbia and Snake rivers.

Two World's Fairs were held in Washington. In 1962 the "Century 21" World's Fair was held in Seattle. Countries from around the world had exhibits there. In 1974 Spokane hosted Expo '74, another World's Fair.

The world's eyes turned to Washington again in 1980. After lying quietly for over 100 years, the volcano at Mount St. Helens erupted. The top of Mount St. Helens was ripped away. Many people were killed by the heat of the blast. Trees were knocked down like toothpicks. Volcanic smoke and ash turned the sky as dark as night for miles around.

Volcano at Mount St. Helens erupts

Berdeen and Green lakes below Bacon Peak looking toward Picket Range

You have learned about some of Washington's history. Now it is time to take a trip—in words and pictures— through the Evergreen State.

Washington is beautiful. It has a lovely coast along the Pacific Ocean. It has green forests ... snow-capped mountains ... blue rivers and lakes ... golden fields of wheat.

In an airplane going east to west, you'll get a good view of the state. You see a lot of farms in the east. You also pass over some mountains and hills. But in the central part of the state you fly over taller, snow-capped peaks. Most of the big cities in Washington are in the west, near the waters of Puget Sound.

Seattle Freeway, Space Needle in background

Seattle is the largest city in Washington. It is on Puget Sound.

In 1851 some settlers from Illinois moved here. They named the town after Chief Seattle. He was a friendly Duwamish (duh • WAWM • ish) Indian chief. Trees were chopped down. Seattle soon became a lumber town. "We have found a valley that will support a thousand families!" said Arthur Denny, who led the settlers to Seattle.

Space Needle and Mount Rainier

What would Denny think if he saw Seattle now? Today, over a *million* people live in Seattle and nearby suburbs. About two of every five people in the whole state live in the Seattle area.

Seattle is a lovely city. Washington's highest peak—Mount Rainier—can be seen to the southeast.

Today, Seattle is a big manufacturing city. The Boeing Company builds 747 jets. Ships are also built in Seattle. Being on Puget Sound makes Seattle a big fishing city, too. Fish are canned in Seattle. Many products are shipped from the Port of Seattle.

Above: Pacific Science Center at the Seattle Center
Right: Space Needle and downtown Seattle

The Seattle Center has buildings left from the
"Century 21" World's Fair. The Space Needle is one of
those buildings. From the 607-foot tower, you can get a
good view of the city. The Pacific Science Center—also
built during the World's Fair—is a science museum. An
opera house, a theater, and an art museum are also in the
Seattle Center. A monorail railroad connects the Seattle
Center with downtown Seattle. This railroad runs on one
rail about fifteen feet above the city.

You can see some of Seattle's past. In 1889 a fire burned down much of the city. Seattle was rebuilt. Part of the old city was left *under* the new city that was built above it. At the waterfront, you can go underground and see that old city.

Seattle is home to the University of Washington. It is the largest college in the Pacific Northwest.

Seattle is a big sports city. The Seahawks play football there. The Mariners play baseball. The SuperSonics play basketball. Sounders play soccer. All the teams play in an indoor stadium called the Kingdome.

Kingdome

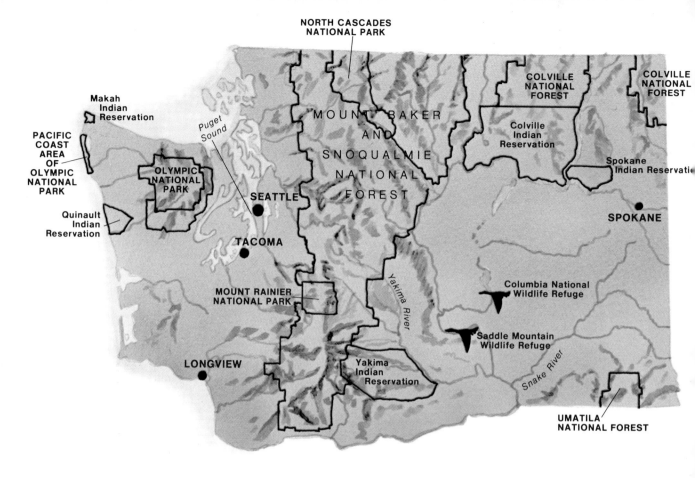

Tacoma is the third largest city in Washington. It is south of Seattle. Tacoma lies on a part of Puget Sound known as Commencement (kuh • MENCE • ment) Bay.

The first explorer here was the Englishman George Vancouver. He explored the region in 1792. Tacoma began as a lumbering town in about 1852.

Today, Tacoma is still a lumber city. Trees are cut down in nearby forests. They are made into furniture in Tacoma. Fishing boats are also made in the city.

The Washington State Historical Society museum is in Tacoma. There, you can learn about Indians and pioneers. If you'd rather be outside, go to Point Defiance (dih • FYE • ence) Park. It has a zoo and an aquarium. Tacoma also has a 105-foot Indian totem pole. It was carved by Indians from Alaska.

The Tacoma Narrows Bridge is over a mile long. It replaced a bridge known as "Galloping Gertie." Galloping Gertie earned that nickname by swaying so much in the wind. A storm smashed Galloping Gertie in 1940.

Olympia is the capital of Washington. It is about 30 miles southwest of Tacoma. It is also a port city on Puget Sound. The Nisqually (niss • KWALL • ee) Indians called this area the "place of the bear." The Olympic Mountains—which include Olympus—are not far from Olympia.

Mount Olympus

Olympia was founded in 1848. It became a lumbering town. In 1853 Olympia became capital of the Washington Territory. When Washington became a state in 1889, Olympia remained as capital.

Visit the Legislative Building in Olympia. It is the state capitol building. There, lawmakers make laws for the Evergreen State. The dome of the capitol building is one of the tallest in the world. The lovely capitol grounds have Japanese cherry trees and beautiful gardens.

State Capitol

Olympia is a small city—only about 30,000 people. Many of the people in the city work for the state government.

Olympia is also known for seafood. Olympia oysters are gathered and canned in Olympia. Beer is brewed in Olympia. Products made in Olympia leave the state from the Olympia harbor.

Bellevue (BELL • vyoo) is the state's fourth largest city. It is a new, fast-growing city.

The city of Everett (EV • ret) is north of Bellevue. Ships are built there. Airplanes are also made nearby.

Commercial fishing boats use nets to bring in their catch.

Puget Sound and the Pacific Ocean help make western Washington a big fishing area. Washington is famous for its salmon.

The salmon are born in the streams and rivers of Washington. The young salmon swim down the rivers into the Pacific Ocean. They live most of their lives in the ocean. But when they are ready to lay eggs, they swim back to the rivers where they were born. It can take months for the salmon to get back to their home rivers.

Above: Sockeye salmon
Left: Salmon fishing attracts many sportsmen.

Fishermen try to catch salmon when the fish leave the ocean on their way to their home streams. Many salmon are caught in Puget Sound. Salmon are canned in Seattle and other fishing cities. Other sea foods that come from Washington include halibut, crabs, clams, oysters, and shrimps. Fish caught in Alaska are also sent down to Seattle for canning.

After visiting these big cities head east into the Cascade (cass • KAID) Mountains. The Cascades were formed by volcanoes, long ago. Red hot liquid rock called lava (LAH • vah) boiled out of the earth. The lava

Tourists hike toward Mount Rainier

hardened, forming the mountains. One mountain in the Cascades, Mount Rainier, is 14,410 feet tall. It is the tallest peak in the state. It is part of Mount Rainier National Park.

Once, Mount Rainier was even taller than it is now. Long ago, a mighty explosion blew the top off Mount Rainier. Steam still seeps out of the mountain. The volcano is "sleeping" now. But some time in the future Mount Rainier may explode again.

The Indians called Mount Rainier the *Mountain that was God.*

The English explorer George Vancouver named it Mount Rainier—after a friend. Later, American explorers tried to climb Mt. Rainier. Some died trying. In 1870 General Hazard Stevens and P.B. Van Trump became the first men known to climb to the top.

Mount Rainier has glaciers that are hundreds of years old. Melting ice from the glaciers feeds waterfalls and streams. Colorful wildflowers grow near the glaciers. In the forests of Mount Rainier National Park there are deer, bears, and beavers. Mountain goats are there, too. There are trails and guides in the park.

The Cascade Mountains have other beautiful peaks, too. You can see glaciers, forests, and wildlife in the areas of Mount Baker and Glacier Peak.

Iceberg Lake and Mount Baker in the North Cascade Survey

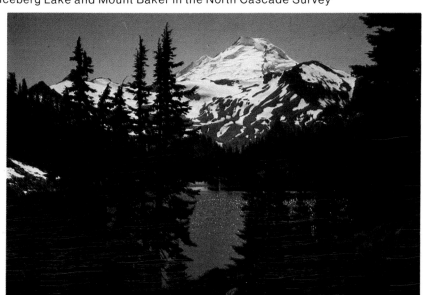

Many of Washington's forests are in the mountains. Washington is one of the leading lumbering states. You remember that loggers cut down whole forests. They did not plant new ones. By 1950, some of Washington's forests were gone. New forests were planted. Today, new trees are planted when old ones are cut.

Loggers aren't the only ones who enjoy Washington's forests and waters. Deer, elk, mountain lions, bobcats, and mountain goats live in the forests and mountains. Red foxes, coyotes, porcupines, and rattlesnakes also live

Above: Elk

Right: Black bear

Above: Sea otter
Left: Beaver

in Washington. Once the beavers were hunted in great
numbers for their fur. Beavers were almost wiped out.
Now laws protect beavers. Today many beavers swim
and build dams in Washington streams.

Laws also protect sea otters. Many, many friendly
otters were killed for fur. Now they can be seen in
waters near the Pacific shore. Dolphins, too, can be seen
swimming off the shore. Now and then, whales swim into
Puget Sound.

Great blue herons, pelicans, gulls, cranes, ducks, and
geese are among the birds living in Washington.

East of the Cascade Mountains you'll see many farms. The main fruit-growing area of Washington is the valleys in the central part of the state. You'll see many apple orchards near the Wenatchee (weh • NOT • chee), Okanogan, and Yakima rivers. Washington is the leading apple-growing state.

Think of Washington the next time you eat a pear, too. Washington is one of the leading pear-growing states.

In fact, many foods come from Washington. Apricots, plums, and berries are other fruits grown in Washington. Potatoes, sweet corn, and green beans are vegetables that are grown. Beef cattle are raised for meat. Dairy cattle are raised for milk.

Washington is also the leading grower of hops. Hops fruits grow on vines. Hops are used to make beer.

As you go farther east in Washington you'll see field after field of wheat. Washington is one of the five leading wheat-growing states in America.

Grand Coulee Dam

Visit Grand Coulee Dam, the second largest producer of power in the world. It is on the Columbia River. This concrete dam is taller than a 40-story building. It is the biggest piece of stone-work ever built by man. The dam helps store the waters of the Columbia River. The water is sent to farms where it is needed. Other dams in Washington include the Chief Joseph Dam, Bonneville (BON • ih • vill) Dam, and the Rock Island Dam.

The second biggest city in Washington—Spokane—is in the far eastern part of the state. It lies on the Spokane River. A waterfall—Spokane Falls—is inside the city. Long ago, the Spokane Indians set up their tepees by the waterfall. Fur traders came here. A fur trading post called Spokane House was built in 1810. The town that grew up here was named Spokane Falls. In 1889 Spokane Falls was destroyed by fire, just like Seattle. The town was rebuilt and named Spokane.

Spokane

Logging truck in western Washington

Spokane is still a trading center. It is part of the *Inland Empire.* This "empire" includes eastern Washington and parts of Idaho, Oregon, and Montana. Trains and highways in the Inland Empire lead to Spokane. Wheat and other farm crops are brought there. Many food products are processed in Spokane. Lumber is brought there, too. The lumber is turned into wood products. These products are then sent from Spokane to other parts of the United States.

Aluminum is processed in Spokane. Aluminum is a metal. It goes into making chewing gum wrappers, pop cans, and parts for airplanes. Spokane's output and that of Bellingham have made Washington the leading aluminum-making state.

Nez Percé dancers at a Folklife Festival

At the Pacific Northwest Indian Center in Spokane you can learn about Indians.

There are over 33,000 Indians from at least 26 tribes in Washington state. About half of the Indians live on reservations. There are 22 reservations in Washington.

Today, Indians have 45 per cent of the privately-owned timber in Washington. They run their own businesses. They cut, sell, and ship the lumber themselves. Indians also own about half the fisheries in Washington. They catch the fish. Then they package and sell it. Indians also work as teachers, doctors, and at other jobs.

Indian dancers perform at Tillicum Village, a North Coast Indian cultural center, on Blake Island

Much of the old Indian culture is alive. Many Indians speak their old language as well as English. Ancient songs, dances, and stories are passed on to young people. Many old customs are followed. There are still "naming ceremonies" at which children are named. Presents are given and a feast is held, as in days of old.

You can't leave Washington without going to Walla Walla in southeast Washington. To the Indians, *Walla Walla* meant *place of many waters*. There are many streams in the area.

Walla Walla is near the place where the Whitmans were killed by Indians. Later, Governor Stevens met with Indians here. There is a statue of Chief Lawyer in Walla Walla. He saved Stevens' life.

Above: Fairy Pool, Mount Rainier
Left: Cape Alava Seashore

Land of beautiful Mount Rainier ... forests ... and ocean waters...

Home to Chief Seattle ... Marcus Whitman ... and Chief Lawyer...

A state of man-made wonders ... the Grand Coulee Dam ... the Space Needle ... and the Seattle monorail...

Manufacturer of airplanes ... ships ... and aluminum...

A wheat, pear, and milk-producing state ... *the* leading apple-growing state....

This is Washington—the Evergreen State.

Facts About WASHINGTON

Area—68,192 square miles (20th biggest state)

Greatest Distance North to South—240 miles

Greatest Distance East to West—358 miles

Borders—Canada to the north; Idaho on the east; Oregon on the south; the Pacific Ocean to the west

Highest Point—14,410 feet above sea level (Mount Rainier)

Lowest Point—Sea level, along the shore of the Pacific Ocean

Hottest Recorded Temperature—118° (near Wahluke on July 24, 1928, and at Ice Harbor Dam on August 5, 1961)

Coldest Recorded Temperature—Minus 48° (at Winthrop and Mazama on the same day, December 30, 1968)

Statehood—42nd state, on November 11, 1889

Origin of Name Washington—After our first president, George Washington

Capital—Olympia

Counties—39

U.S. Senators—2

U.S. Representatives—2

Electoral Votes—9

State Senators—49

State Representatives—98

State Song—"Washington, My Home" by Helen Davis

State Motto—*Alki* (a Chinook Indian word that means "Bye and bye")

Nicknames—Evergreen State, Chinook State

State Seal—Adopted in 1889

State Flag—Adopted in 1925

State Flower—Coast rhododendron

State Bird—Willow goldfinch

State Tree—Western hemlock

State Gem—Petrified wood

State Colors—Green and gold

Principal River—Columbia

Some Other Rivers—Snake, Okanogan, Spokane, Yakima, Wenatchee, Skagit, Pend Oreille, Cowlitz, Noohack

Indian Reservations—22

National Forests—9

National Parks—3 (Mount Rainier, North Cascades, and Olympic national parks)

Some Lakes—Franklin D. Roosevelt Lake, Lake Chelan, Moses Lake, Lake Washington

Some Waterfalls—Fairy, Narada, Sluiskin, Rainbow, Cascade, Spokane

Some Mountain Peaks—Mount Rainier, Mount Adams, Mount Baker, Glacier Peak, Mount St. Helens, Mount Olympus

Farm Products—Wheat, apples, pears, cherries, plums, apricots, hops, beans, peas, barley, sweet corn, asparagus, sugar beets, potatoes, milk, beef cattle, sheep

Fishing—Salmon, halibut, flounder, trout, cod, shrimp, whitefish, tuna, oysters, crabs, clams, herring, sturgeon

Wildlife—Deer, elk, bears, beavers, minks, bobcats, pheasants, quail, ducks, geese, porcupines, gophers, garter snakes, bull snakes, rattlesnakes, dolphins, sea otters, whales, mountain lions, coyotes, flying squirrels

Mining—Coal, uranium, copper, gold, silver, zinc

Manufacturing Products—Airplanes, ships, wood products, paper products, processed foods, aluminum, metal products, clothes, chemicals

Population—3,544,000 (1975 estimate)

Major Cities—

City	Population	
Seattle	470,000	(all 1979 estimates)
Spokane	176,900	
Tacoma	155,100	
Bellevue	69,800	
Lakewood Center	51,400	
Yakima	51,100	
Everett	49,500	
Vancouver	49,000	

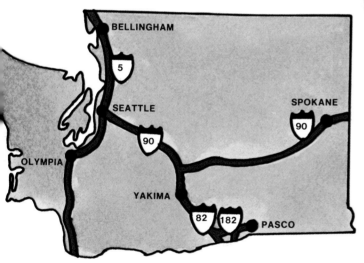

Washington's History

There were people in Washington at least 10,000 years ago, probably much longer.

1592—The man called Juan de Fuca, working for the king of Spain, possibly sails along the Washington coast in this year

1774—Juan Perez sails along coast for Spain and sees Mt. Olympus

1775—Heceta and Quadra become first explorers known to walk on Washington soil; they claim land for Spain

1778—Captain James Cook explores coast for England

1792—American Captain Robert Gray names Columbia River

1792-1794—English Captain George Vancouver explores Washington coast and claims area for king of England

1805—Lewis and Clark explore area for United States

1810—English trading post Spokane House is founded by North West Fur Company

1811—Fort Okanogan, first American settlement in Washington, is founded

1818—England and United States agree that people from both countries can trade and live in Washington

1825—Dr. John McLoughlin rules at Fort Vancouver for English

1836—Marcus Whitman founds mission near Walla Walla

1843—Large numbers of people come west on Oregon Trail

1845—American town of Tumwater is founded

1846—After England and U.S. argue about boundaries, Washington becomes part of United States

1847—Cayuse Indians kill Marcus and Narcissa Whitman and a number of others at mission

1848—Washington is part of Oregon Territory, which belongs to U.S.

1852—Seattle is founded

1853—Washington Territory is formed; only 3,965 settlers live there

1855-1858—Indian Wars

1859—United States and England argue over boundaries during "Pig War"

1861—University of Washington is founded

1870—Population is 23,355

1871—Beginning of city of Spokane

1880—Population is 75,116

1883—Railroad crosses Washington

1889—Washington becomes our 42nd state on November 11; Seattle and Spokane have fires in this year

1890—Population is 337,232

1892—Washington State University opens

1897—During Gold Rush to Alaska, prospectors stop at Seattle

1899—Mount Rainier National Park is created

1900—Population is 518,103

1904—Bing Crosby is born in Tacoma

1910—Women obtain right to vote in Washington

1914-1918—During World War I, 67,694 Washington men and 632 women are in uniform

1920—Population is 1,356,621

1928—Capitol building in Olympia is finished

1938—Olympic National Park is created

1939-1945—World War II; Hanford Works helps create atomic bomb

1942—Grand Coulee Dam is completed

1943—First atomic energy plant opens in Hanford

1946—Construction of Columbia Irrigation Project begins

1950—Work is begun on Chief Joseph Dam

1950—Tacoma Narrows Bridge is completed, replacing "Galloping Gertie"
1962—"Century 21" World's Fair is held in Seattle
1967—Boeing Company opens big airplane plant near Everett
1970—Population is 3,409,169
1974—Expo '74 World's Fair is held in Spokane
1976—The Kingdome—a domed sports stadium—opens
1977—Dixy Lee Ray is the first woman governor of Washington
1980—Mount St. Helens becomes an active volcano

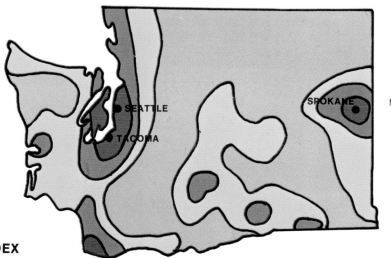

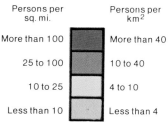

Persons per sq. mi.		Persons per km²	
More than 100		More than 40	
25 to 100		10 to 40	
10 to 25		4 to 10	
Less than 10		Less than 4	

INDEX

47

INDEX, Cont'd

About the Author:

Dennis Fradin attended Northwestern University on a creative writing scholarship and graduated in 1967. While still at Northwestern, he published his first stories in *Ingenue* magazine and also won a prize in *Seventeen's* short story competition. A prolific writer, Dennis Fradin has been regularly publishing stories in such diverse places as *The Saturday Evening Post, Scholastic, National Humane Review, Midwest,* and *The Teaching Paper.* He has also scripted several educational films. Since 1970 he has taught second grade reading in a Chicago school—a rewarding job, which, the author says, "provides a captive audience on whom I test my children's stories." Married and the father of three children, Dennis Fradin spends his free time with his family or playing a myriad of sports and games with his childhood chums.

About the Artists:

Len Meents studied painting and drawing at Southern Illinois University and after graduation in 1969 he moved to Chicago. Mr. Meents works full time as a painter and illustrator. He and his wife and child currently make their home in LaGrange, Illinois.

Richard Wahl, graduate of the Art Center College of Design in Los Angeles, has illustrated a number of magazine articles and booklets. He is a skilled artist and photographer who advocates realistic interpretations of his subjects. He lives with his wife and two sons in Libertyville, Illinois.

48